Original title:
Two Souls, One Destiny

Author: Hannah Garcia
ISBN HARDBACK: 978-9908-0-0980-3
ISBN PAPERBACK: 978-9908-0-0981-0

Guided by the Same North Star

In a sky of glittering light,
We both laugh at our clumsy flight.
Each wrong turn brings a funny tale,
Together we wander, we never fail.

With maps made of crumpled dreams,
Navigating through each other's schemes.
Though lost, we dance in the rain,
Spinning round, it's never plain.

Echoes of Fate

Life sends us on a quirky ride,
Where banter and laughter collide.
Every twist, a chuckle or two,
Your punchlines are my favorite view.

With each look, confusion subsides,
Our mismatch, a source of great pride.
We giggle at fate's silly game,
Waddling through life, never the same.

The Firefly Connection

In the night, we glow and blink,
A dance of light makes us think.
With every flicker, a giggly cheer,
We stumble close, then disappear.

Chasing sparks with all our might,
Two goofballs lost in twilight.
A tangled mess of heartfelt whim,
Our laughter fills the air to brim.

Threads of Light

Stitching tales with threads of cheer,
We weave laughter, have no fear.
Each tug pulls us closer still,
In this fabric of fun, we thrill.

With colors bright and patterns wild,
Life's tapestry plays tricks like a child.
Every seam a chance to tease,
Together we float on a gentle breeze.

In the Embrace of Starlit Promise

Under the moon's cheeky grin,
We dance like pinballs, full of spin.
With each tumble, laughter's our guide,
In a comedy club, our hearts collide.

Stars wink at our silly plight,
Catching us in their twinkling light.
Falling over, we beam with glee,
An orbit of joy, just you and me.

The Unbreakable Bond of Time

Like socks lost in the dryer's doom,
Our paths twist anyway, with room.
Through ticking clocks, we prank the fate,
Time's just a playground for our date.

In the toaster, we pop and toast,
Running late, but we laugh the most.
We flip the calendar with a wink,
Two goofballs, too bold to rethink.

Echoes of Love in Parallel Worlds

In a universe of jellybeans,
You wear a crown made of greens.
We chase rainbows in silly shoes,
Sipping soda, what's there to lose?

Every giggle bends the space,
Creating chaos with a smiley face.
From galaxies far, we take a ride,
In laughter's arms, forever abide.

A Journey Beyond the Veil

Through curtains of mist, we sneak and peek,
Finding treasures in every squeak.
With potions brewed from tangerine,
Our mischief sparkles, oh so keen!

In this realm of slapstick play,
We cartwheel through the light of day.
With every giggle, we break the mold,
Adventures unfolding, bold and gold.

The Union of Spirits

In a café, they both sat tight,
One liked dark, the other light.
They stirred their cups with glee and grins,
While debating on who had more wins.

Their lifelines twisted, a comical mess,
Mixing up names and dates, nonetheless.
With laughter ringing through the day,
They'd often get lost in words that stray.

They danced through chaos, side by side,
Trading jokes and laughter as their guide.
With each blunder, their hearts did swell,
A radiant bond, who could tell?

In this wild waltz of fate's delight,
They found joy in every silly fight.
For in this duo, so stark and bright,
Life's absurdities felt just right.

The Pulse of Eternity

Beating hearts that skip a beat,
When they compete for the last sweet treat.
She grabbed the pie, he made a face,
Yet he'd still run, just to keep pace.

They shared a glance, then burst in laughter,
Over who could dance better, chorus or after.
With moves so quirky, they spun around,
Until someone tripped, and down they found.

In a world of snacks and embarrassing fun,
Each moment felt like a race to be won.
With silly bets and goofy jests,
They made a home in laughter's nests.

Side by side, like mischief and mirth,
In their playful chaos, they found worth.
With every giggle, every silly spree,
Their lives entwined—perfect harmony.

Sandy Footprints of Affection

On a beach where waves collide,
They buried their worries, took joy as a ride.
With sand in their toes and laughter in air,
They built wobbly castles, without a care.

As seagulls joked and critters played near,
They tossed salty water, full of cheer.
With wrinkled brows and sunshine smiles,
They made up games that lasted for miles.

Their footprints danced like a wiggly worm,
As they chased the tide, with a giggle and turn.
Each splash and stumble a hilarious sight,
Under the sun, everything felt right.

With sandy hair and salty skin,
They knew this bond was the best kind of win.
For in every grain of laughter shared,
Lies a magic connection that's truly rare.

Timeless Connection

In a time machine made of cheese,
We giggle like squirrels in the trees.
Sharing secrets with the moon,
Juggling stars to a silly tune.

Our hearts beat like a disco ball,
Bouncing laughter in the hall.
For every time we trip and fall,
A cosmic dance unites us all.

The Language of Us

We speak in winks and silly grins,
Like penguins wearing goofy fins.
Your laugh's a melody that's sweet,
A cosmic rhythm, light on feet.

With dance moves like a wobbly duck,
Together, we squeak out of luck.
A secret code of rhymes and fun,
Writing stories just us, two in one.

Luminaries of Love

You're the peanut to my jelly,
Twirling freely like a silly belly.
We shine bright like a disco star,
Riding rainbows in a candy car.

Chasing giggles through the night,
You hold my heart, it's pure delight.
In a world that's upside down,
Together, we wear the silliest crown.

Celestial Underpinnings

In a galaxy filled with cheese,
Our laughter floats upon the breeze.
Orbiting joy, a merry spree,
Two clowns playing, wild and free.

With cosmic pies and comet zest,
We turn the universe to a jest.
All the stars in perfect glee,
Winking at us, can't you see?

Echoes of Togetherness

In a world of mismatched socks,
We dance on sidewalks, avoiding rocks.
Your laugh is a serenade, so bright,
As we trip on shadows, what a sight!

Coffee spilled on my favorite book,
You steal my fries with a sly look.
Together we bumble, side by side,
With giggles that burst like popcorn fried.

Our GPS leads us wayward and lost,
Yet each wrong turn is worth the cost.
In silly moments, we find our way,
Like rain or shine, we laugh and play.

So here's to our chaos, wild and free,
A tapestry woven of you and me.
In this charming mess, we've found our song,
With echoes of togetherness all along.

A Journey Shared

With snacks packed tight for the road ahead,
We set off laughing, no fear, no dread.
You're the queen of Google, I'm the map,
Together we're tangled, what a mishap!

An old car breaks down, what a delight!
We're camped in a puddle, laughing at night.
With stories and jokes, our fuel not in gas,
Every mile is a treasure, let's raise a glass!

From city lights to forest trails wide,
Side by side, we take every stride.
Your silly dance makes the stops worthwhile,
Road tripping together brings the best smile.

As we ride through life, let's steer with glee,
For adventures await, just you and me.
Each bump in the road, we cuppa and share,
In this journey together, nothing can compare.

The Whispering Winds of Fate

On a breezy day, we met at the park,
You chased a pigeon, and it left quite a mark.
With outbursts of laughter and playful chases,
We spun under trees, forgettable places.

Like ice cream cones that melt in the sun,
We make each moment a crazy fun run.
With mud on our shoes, we dance and twirl,
Each gust that blows brings giggles and whirl.

The whispers of nature, they tell our tale,
Of wild capers and hearts that won't fail.
Through trees and breeze, we forge the way,
In this absurd play, let's frolic and sway.

So let the winds carry our laughter wide,
For in this wacky world, we'll always glide.
As fate unfolds, side by side we'll be,
In every breeze, just you and me.

Mirrored Reflections

In the mirror, we see double the fun,
Two quirky faces, under the sun.
Your silly grin gives my heart a boost,
Together our giggles, we let them loose.

Like reflections in water, we ripple and glow,
Twisting and turning, just putting on a show.
When one trips and stumbles, the other will laugh,
In this waltz of clumsiness, we find our path.

With jokes that bounce like a rubber ball,
We chase after dreams, we'd never drop the call.
Through mirrored moments, oh so absurd,
Our laughter echoes, it's truly unheard.

So let's paint our story with colors so bright,
In the gallery of life, we'll shine in the night.
Every slip and slide, we'll cherish and keep,
For in this funny dance, our bond runs deep.

Embrace of the Infinite

In a café, they both sat down,
Spilling coffee, wearing a frown.
Each bite of cake, a giggle loud,
Their clumsiness drew a laughing crowd.

Tangled in their silly fate,
Tripping over chairs, oh what a state!
They chuckled at the chaos grown,
In every misstep, a love was sown.

With muffins flying, they took a chance,
Dancing on tables, a silly dance.
Two forks clinked, a cheerful clatter,
Life's little mess made love even fatter.

As sunlight fades, their laughter starts,
In the day's end, they stole each other's hearts.
Life's goofy moments, they both embraced,
In the endless joy, their lives interlaced.

Chords of Fate

A ukulele strums, off-key delight,
With every note, they hope to take flight.
Together they laugh, a rhythm so odd,
Playing love songs to a wiggly cod.

They danced in circles, stepped on each toe,
Creating a symphony, a wacky show.
With each little glance, something new played,
Life's been a jam session, a serenade.

A picnic blanket, snacks all askew,
Spilled lemonade mixed with a shoe.
Yet laughter rang loud above the sound,
In every blunder, their love was found.

When the music fades, they find their beat,
Two hearts together, an off-tune feat.
Through every quirk, every silly note,
Love strummed their chords, it kept them afloat.

Divinely Meant

In a line for pizza, they caught each other's eye,
As toppings fell, they burst into a sigh.
Sauce on their shirts, they just couldn't quit,
Each silly mishap was a perfect fit.

With cheesy jokes, they shared a glance,
Lost in laughter, a delightful dance.
Two slices shared, a silly sight,
In the pepperoni, love bloomed bright.

Stargazing under a pizza-shaped moon,
Singing off-key, a glorious tune.
They laughed at the stars, so far away,
Yet felt each other, come what may.

When pizza rolls in, they dance with glee,
In their funny world, just meant to be.
With every bite, their hearts would ring,
In the warmth of laughter, they'd always sing.

Synchronized Hearts

In a dance class, they both stepped wrong,
Tripping together, a clumsy throng.
With twirls and spins, they'd flip and flop,
Everyone laughed, they just couldn't stop.

They practiced moves with a silly flair,
Their rhythm a mess, but they didn't care.
Hearts in sync, amidst the stray feet,
Their goofy twirls turned chaos to sweet.

On the floor, they rolled like two clowns,
Falling in giggles, ignoring the frowns.
With every stumble, a bond so tight,
In laughter and dance, they found their light.

As music fades, they bow with pride,
A goofy love that won't ever hide.
In every step, a harmony shines,
Together in dance, their love intertwines.

A Symphony for the Beloved

In a world where squirrels dance,
Their acorns play a merry tune.
You clapped your hands in jest,
While I was stuck in a raccoon.

A song off-key, but oh so bright,
You twirled me round, I lost my shoe.
With laughter echoing through the night,
We stepped on toes, but who cares? You!

A cat joined in, all silk and sass,
It joined our band, we set the stage.
Conclusion? There's no need to pass,
This symphony is love, age to age.

So let the world be our grand hall,
We'll laugh and tiptoe, side by side.
For in this dance, we have it all,
With you, my muse, I can't abide.

Destined to Wander Together

We roam the streets with ice cream cones,
I dropped mine in a puddle, oh dear!
You laughed so hard, it broke the stones,
Then tripped on air, my laughter near.

The pigeons are judging, you swear they do,
While we stumble through the park, quite a sight.
With you, life's a movie, a silly crew,
Chasing after each other, our hearts feel light.

Let's venture forth, get lost in the maze,
We'll read the map upside down for fun.
Our adventure's wild, the whole world's our stage,
And every wrong turn sparks another run.

So here's to wandering, at least we meet,
In laughter's grip, we can't be beat.
Together we'll chase all life's treats,
For wandering souls can't feel defeat!

The Unseen Thread of Connection

Tangled threads, we weave a spell,
In every laugh, in every clink.
You wear mismatched socks so well,
Together, we're already on the brink.

A wink, a nudge, a shared dessert,
Your fork's now mine, it's a great swap.
With humor bright, we'll never hurt,
The candy store's our favorite stop.

Invisible strings pull us around,
Like puppets dancing in a show.
With every misstep, we're still spellbound,
And in our antics, oh, how we glow!

So here's to laughter, sweet and light,
With every mishap, we take flight.
Together, we craft joy overnight,
And dance our way into the night.

Love's Journey Through the Ages

We started off in cardboard cars,
Your steering wheel made of old tin cans.
Zooming through the interstellar bars,
In capes and masks, we made our plans.

The years rolled on, we found new games,
From hide and seek to joke-telling quests.
We donned mustaches, we played with names,
Creating chaos, we were the best.

Adventure called, we took the leap,
With popcorn fights and late-night snacks.
Each joke we cracked, each secret we keep,
Together we blend, love never lacks.

So here's to us, forever young,
With hearts that giggle and always play.
Through all life's stages, we've just begun,
Navigating on our goofy way.

Serendipity's Woven Path

In a crowded café, a spill on the floor,
They met over coffee, both yelling, "No more!"
With laughter like bubbles, they stuck like glue,
A clumsy romance that only they knew.

A dog stole their lunch, what a sight to behold,
They chased after it laughing, not caring or cold.
With every misstep, their connection grew tight,
Two jokers in love, what a hilarious plight.

At a dance-off near city lights all aglow,
They tripped on each other, but oh what a show!
With two left feet, they still managed to groove,
Fate's silly way of making them move.

Now on their grand journey, they wear matching shoes,
With mismatched socks, they couldn't care to lose.
In life's foolish moments, they find their way,
Laughing together, come what may.

Dance of the Twin Flames

In a disco ball's shimmer, they met by chance,
Two awkward dancers who couldn't quite prance.
With every misstep, they fell to the ground,
But laughter erupted, a sweet, funny sound.

They twirled in a whirlwind of fabric and hair,
Each movement a fluke, but they didn't care.
With every slip, they invented new moves,
Creating their rhythm, their own silly grooves.

A sudden slip led to spontaneous spins,
They ended up laughing from chins to their grins.
Beneath flashing lights, their mishaps a tease,
Their hearts did the tango, a dance to appease.

And as they kept dancing, the chemistry soared,
No need for perfection, they both were adored.
With joyous abandon, they laughed and they played,
In a dance of pure bliss, their worries allayed.

The Light that Mends the Fractured

In a world full of blunders, they were the glue,
With hilarious moments, their journey was true.
They stumbled at dinner, a splash of red wine,
Creating a masterpiece, oh how divine!

A borrowed umbrella turned into a kite,
They floated through storms, hearts soaring in flight.
With each silly mishap, their bond only grew,
Two goofballs together, together they flew.

On a foggy day, they pretended to race,
The finish line? Laughter, not a single trace.
With giggles aplenty, they painted the gray,
Their light rained cheer on a dull, dreary day.

So here's to the blunders that made them a pair,
Their laughter contagious, a love most rare.
In this tale of mishaps, forever they'll shine,
Turning fumbles to magic, their hearts are entwined.

Hearts Interlaced Through Space

In a cosmic dance, they stumbled through stars,
Bumping into comets and crashing their cars.
With laughter like meteors, they lit up the night,
Two clumsy adventurers, holding on tight.

Each galaxy found them in fits of delight,
With moonbeams and giggles, they took flight.
A trip to the planets? Oh, what a blunder!
Yet in their sweet chaos, they fell into wonder.

With every supernova, they played and they clashed,
Creating their magic, two hearts full-thrashed.
Through black holes and wormholes, adventure to trace,
They laughed through their journeys, time and space.

So here's to the moments that make love a blast,
With humor as fuel, they secured their bond fast.
In the vastness of space, they've found their own grace,
Interlaced through this cosmos, their joyous embrace.

Convergence of Stars

In a galaxy far, far away,
Where puppies wear shades and cats play,
Two comets collide with a bang and a cheer,
Leaving trails of laughter, oh dear, oh dear!

Asteroids dance to a silly tune,
While aliens wobble on a big yellow balloon,
They share giggles under a cosmic dome,
A party in space, far away from home!

With cosmic cake and astrodust cupcakes,
They toast with starlight, for goodness' sakes,
As planets spin around in a dizzy whirl,
Galactic giggles make the universe twirl!

So here's to the twinkling cosmic delight,
Where strange creatures party all through the night,
For in the end, it's all just one big show,
A wacky reunion of stars all aglow!

Union Beyond Time

In a realm where clocks just can't tick,
A monkey wears glasses, and it's quite a trick,
Two friends decided to mess with fate,
They thought, 'Let's be late! You can't be too straight!'

They flew past the past and cavorted with gnomes,
In a forest filled with oversized homes,
Sipping tea with a dragon, they shared a good joke,
While time stood still, as wise as a bloke.

With a wink and a grin, they rolled through the skies,
Counting clouds in the shape of pies,
Every second a giggle, every minute a dance,
Finding joy in the chaos, what a happenstance!

Back and forth through the giggles of hours,
They planted dreams like blooming flowers,
In a universe painted with laughter and rhyme,
Together they proved that there's no end to time!

Luminous Hearts Entwined

In a land where rubber ducks like to race,
Two bright hearts met in a whimsical place,
They laughed as they twirled on candy-coated grass,
Chasing jellybeans, oh what a class!

With beaming smiles and glittery flair,
They built a castle made of fresh air,
They knotted their wishes with some silly string,
Crafting a future where joy is the king!

A unicorn pranced, joined in their fun,
Sipping hot cocoa beneath a warm sun,
With pies in the sky and clouds made of fluff,
They danced in harmony, that's just enough!

Their laughter echoed, a song of delight,
Two luminous beings shining so bright,
In a world where humor forever entwines,
Creating a symphony where love truly shines!

Serendipity's Embrace

Oh, what a surprise, they bumped on the street,
A penguin and puppy, what a quirky meet!
With a flap and a wag, they hatched a plan,
To start a parade led by a sandwich grand!

With confetti made of sprinkles and cheer,
They danced through the city, with no fear,
Singing silly songs, stealing hearts on the way,
In a flash mob of giggles, come join the display!

A tuba player joined, honking so loud,
As the crowds gathered, oh what a crowd!
With puddles of puddin' and jellybeans too,
Their serendipitous journey just grew and grew!

From the bursts of laughter to balloon-dancing dreams,
They realized together, life's better it seems,
In the embrace of joy that never does wane,
Two silly hearts, always up for the game!

Union Beneath a Shared Sky

In a world that spins and twirls,
Two odd socks dance like girls.
One is striped, the other plain,
Together they ignore the rain.

They argue over who's the star,
Yet cozy on a couch, they spar.
With popcorn flying, laughter's prize,
Beneath the same vast, silly skies.

Each day they share their daily eats,
One likes bananas, one likes beets.
They trade their tales of woe and glee,
In this wild comedy, it's plain to see.

Through chores and pranks, they make their way,
Here's to the joy of a shared buffet.
Amidst the chaos, they both agree,
Life's better when there's company.

Harmony in the Echoing Silence

In a quiet room, the cat meows,
While the dog rolls his eyes and vows.
They sip their tea, it's quite a laugh,
As they ponder who's the better staff.

One plays the flute, the other hums,
Creating tunes from silly drumming thumps.
While shushing each, they pull a face,
Echoes of joy in their shared space.

With mismatched socks and goofy hats,
Their conversations bounce like playful cats.
Each odd quirk somehow entwines,
In the echo of their silly signs.

They may not agree on how to play,
But one brings cupcakes to save the day.
Amidst the silence, loud and bright,
Their laughter dances, pure delight.

Bound by the Celestial Tide

As stars aligned in a quirky dance,
One brought snacks, the other took a chance.
They wished on comets from night's cozy chair,
Plotting how to become a bear!

In a universe full of fanciful schemes,
They launch their jokes like crazy dreams.
The moon giggles at this delight,
Cosmic coffee breaks feel so right.

With meteors coming to hear their tales,
They launch into laughter on vibrant trails.
In spaces unknown, the chaos flows,
Two hearts laughing as the tide just grows.

Bound by the currents of sheer fun,
Through cosmic pranks, they've just begun.
Under the stars, what a silly sight,
Their cheerful antics light up the night.

Chasing Shadows of a Shared Dream

From morning rays to evening's sighs,
A duet sung beneath the skies.
They chase shadows at the break of dawn,
While planning how to prank the lawn.

In every game and wild charade,
They jest about the plans they've made.
Jumping into puddles, just to tease,
While aiming for the biggest sneeze.

With dreams as wild as a kite in flight,
They morph into monsters, what a sight!
Their laughter shared, the joy is real,
In these moments, life's a steal.

Together they dream of candy rain,
While breaking barriers with their wacky train.
In a world where shadows leap and bound,
Their silly antics truly astound.

The Heart's Silent Agreement

In a crowded room, they met, just by chance,
With a clumsy smile, they began to dance.
She spilled her drink; it splashed on his shoe,
He laughed so hard, she thought he might too.

Whispers of fate, they giggled and twirled,
As a tumbleweed rolled through their little world.
He stole her fries, she stole his hat,
Together they flourished, imagine that!

Reflections of Fate's Design

Bumping carts in the grocery store,
She grabbed his snack, 'Don't you want more?'
He replied with a wink, 'I'll split the pie,'
While they both dreamed of the taste of the sky.

Playing chess, a strategic fumble,
He lost his queen, she giggled, 'Let's stumble!'
Their laughter echoed, chess pieces astray,
Who knew losing could brighten the day?

Of Moonlight and Shared Desires

Under the stars, they made a toast,
To spaghetti and meatballs—oh, what a boast!
He twirled the noodles, spun them around,
Till her sauce-covered face made quite the sound.

With fireflies buzzing, they danced in the glow,
Tripping on laughter, with one toe on show.
They chased after dreams, like kids on a spree,
Who knew weaving magic could be so carefree?

Love's Guiding Compass

At the park, they lost track of the time,
While chasing ducks, they both felt sublime.
He fell in the pond, she burst into fits,
Wiping her tears, more from the giggles than hits.

As the sun set, they faced a dilemma,
Their ice cream melted, such a sweet enigma!
They shared one cone, tipped over—oh dear!
But nothing could stop their contagious cheer.

Alchemy of Love

In a lab where hearts collide,
Potions bubble, laughter wide.
Mixing giggles, just for fun,
Creating chaos, just begun.

Bubbling brews of coffee shared,
Stirring troubles, none are scared.
A sprinkle of dreams, a dash of cheese,
With every sip, we laugh with ease.

Love's a recipe, odd but sweet,
Unexpected flavors, pure repeat.
With every quirk, we're intertwined,
In this strange kitchen, fate's designed.

Cackling as we spill some spice,
This tangled mess is oh so nice.
Two wacky chefs in blissful glee,
A tasty treat, just you and me!

Beneath the Veil of the Moon

Under the moon, our shadows dance,
Tripping over, who needs a chance?
With every stumble, giggles ring,
Who knew clouds could make us sing?

A serenade of silly tunes,
Howling at the light of the moons.
In every twirl, we lose our way,
But who cares? We're here to play!

Chasing starlight, woes dismissed,
Shouldn't we be on a list?
For the quirkiest duo around,
In the moonlight, laughter's found.

Gravity shifts with every joke,
As we float on dreams we stoke.
Oh what fun, this night is bold,
Together we shine, our tales retold!

Whispers in the Twilight

As shadows stretch and daylight blurs,
We swap our dreams like silly spurts.
Whispers float on twilight air,
And with each giggle, we declare.

Underneath the whispering trees,
We challenge fate with tumbling knees.
The world may laugh, but here we stand,
Imperfect jesters, hand in hand.

The mysterious dusk, our secret stage,
Where awkward stories never age.
With each blunder, we intertwine,
In the twilight, all things align.

Get ready for the jokes to land,
With each punchline, we take a stand.
In the hush of night, our spirits soar,
Together, forever, we always explore!

Radiance of Together

Two misfits in a radiant glow,
Stumbling forth in a comic show.
With socked feet and tangled hair,
We laugh so hard there's joy to spare.

Sharing snacks, our fingers meet,
Catching crumbs while we skip a beat.
In this glow, we create our spark,
As we dance around in the dark.

The world can't help but turn and stare,
At our quirky magic, light as air.
With each bright smile, our hearts collide,
This gleaming bond we cannot hide.

So here's to us, in harmony,
In every mishap, you'll find me.
With laughter ringing, bright and true,
This radiant life: just me and you!

Love's Eternal Bond

In a world so vast and wide,
We trip and fall with silly pride.
Hands held tight, we stumble fast,
Making memories that forever last.

You snore like a bear in deep sleep,
While I count the sheep, not a peep.
With laughter as our daily chore,
Life's comedy, who could ask for more?

In every bicker, every tease,
You still steal my heart with ease.
Through thick and thin, we dance and sway,
In this love, we'll always play.

Partners in mischief, side by side,
A goofy smile, we can't hide.
With every glance, joy cascades,
Together we've got it made.

Chasing Shadows Together

In the sun's glow, we race and spin,
Chasing shadows with a cheeky grin.
You trip on air, I laugh so loud,
In this silly dance, we're forever proud.

With ice cream drips on our faces bright,
We share our hopes with pure delight.
Your jokes are bad, but I laugh anyway,
As we wander through life's playful fray.

We dance in puddles when it rains,
Splashing about, ignoring pains.
In every giggle, we find a spark,
Together we light up the dark.

As shadows stretch, we sway and hum,
Creating tales, oh, where do we come from?
In our little world, the fun won't cease,
Together we find our sweetest peace.

The Symphony of Us

You play the kazoo, I tap the drum,
In our off-key tune, we both feel numb.
With every note, the laughter flows,
In this wild composition, anything goes.

You waltz like a penguin, I spin like a top,
In our quirky dance, we just can't stop.
The world may frown at our clumsy beat,
But in this madness, we feel complete.

Every hiccup becomes a rhyme,
Making melodies that dance through time.
With tickles and grins, we chase the moon,
Our hearts hum a sweet, silly tune.

In this orchestra, you're my best part,
Playing the strings of my funny heart.
As we laugh and sway with delight,
Together, we'll dance into the night.

Hearts in Synchrony

In our goofy ways, we beat as one,
With mismatched socks, we have such fun.
Through silly moments and playful quirks,
Our bond grows strong, like love that works.

You steal my fries, I roll my eyes,
Yet laughter erupts like a sweet surprise.
In every snicker, in every tease,
Together we dance, our hearts at ease.

In the cluttered chaos of our shared space,
We build our dreams with a silly grace.
Like tangled yarn, we twist and twine,
In this tangled mess, your heart's in mine.

With every laugh and goofy jest,
You're my partner and my very best.
Together we sway, in perfect time,
In the rhythm of love, we find our rhyme.

In Synchronicity

In a dance, we twirl around,
With mismatched socks, we're glory-bound.
You trip, I laugh, a comic show,
Yet in each stumble, we steal the glow.

We share a cake, you take the bite,
Guess who ends up with frosting white?
With every joke that makes us roll,
We ride the waves, two hearts as one whole.

Your quirks align with my strange news,
Together we craft our own wild muse.
Through every punchline, side by side,
In this comic chaos, we take pride.

So here's to laughter, our shared delight,
In every mishap, we'll take flight.
For in this life, with all its twists,
You're my partner, through laughter and lists.

The Great Design

In a maze, we wander 'round,
With silly hats, we're glory-bound.
You find the exit, I lose the way,
But together we make it a fun day.

With every map, your sense of fun,
I follow trails where puns are spun.
Through tangled paths, we chase the cheese,
And laugh at fate's little quirks with ease.

Your dance moves mimic a chicken's groove,
But together, oh boy, we make it a move!
With every twirl and silly kick,
We bluster through life, oh so quick!

So let us prance through this grand design,
In goofy steps, we'll always shine.
For in this play, however absurd,
You're my laughter, my heart's best word.

Paths of Destiny

Side by side on life's wide street,
You wear odd shoes, I mismatched feet.
We trip on laughs, we stumble on fate,
Creating memories that resonate.

Through puddles deep and skies of gray,
You splash and grin, come what may.
With each wrong turn, we find delight,
In paths uncharted, we feel just right.

With maps that crinkle, plans in dismay,
We chase the sun, come what may.
With every giggle, we pave our way,
In life's bright circus, we seize the day!

So here's to our journey, a laugh parade,
With every twist, we're unafraid.
Together, we stroll, by whim and chance,
Designing our fate in a silly dance.

Harmonizing Beats

In sync we sway to life's own tune,
With laughter loud, under a silly moon.
You drop the beat, I clap along,
In every rhythm, we both belong.

Your dance is wild, a sight to see,
With a twist and a spin, you're oh so free.
We harmonize in a laugh-fueled craze,
In this quirky duet, forever we blaze.

Through whispered jokes and playful tease,
We find our groove with effortless ease.
With every misstep, we hear the rhyme,
In goofy giggles, we spin through time.

So let's keep dancing, let laughter reign,
In each silly moment, we'll never wane.
For in this life, with hearts in sync,
Together we thrive, in laughter we wink.

Celestial Confluence

In the galaxy of snickers and glee,
Where giggles orbit happily,
Stars dance like they've lost their minds,
Bumping heads, leaving no one behind.

Comets race with a playful twist,
Dropping ice cream, oh what a mist!
Jupiter teases, with rings that swing,
While Mars chuckles at the mess we bring.

Meteor showers of popcorn delight,
Creating a feast under the night.
Planets wink as they whiz on by,
In this cosmic carnival, we'll fly high.

From this chaos, laughter ignites,
In the vastness where joy takes flight,
Together we share the silly jest,
In a universe that knows us best.

The Bridge of Understanding

On a bridge made of jellybeans, we sway,
Tasting each color, come what may.
Balancing laughs like tightrope acts,
With each stumble, we concoct new pacts.

A fervent debate: is blue the best?
Or perhaps the flavors in this zesty quest?
We share our quirks, no need to hide,
In this candy lane, we take a ride.

Underneath rainbows, we giggle and quirk,
Our minds weave stories filled with smirk.
With every hop, our thoughts align,
Building bridges with humor so fine.

Hand in hand, like twizzlers, we tie,
Sprinkling joy as we laugh and cry.
On this confectionary path, we stroll,
Together we bloom, heart and soul.

In Perfect Harmony

In a band where we both play notes,
With silly rhythms that wobble and float.
Strumming on ukuleles with glee,
Our tunes are a blend of you and me.

We dance in socks, making quite a mess,
While giggling at each other's finesse.
The harmony isn't quite on key,
Yet every clap screams, 'Yay, that's us, you see!'

A kazoo chorus breaks the silence wide,
As we mimic fish on an ocean ride.
Two left feet don't bother us much,
Slipping and sliding in our goofy touch.

In this ballad of laughter, we'll sway,
Finding joy in every off-beat play.
With hearts in sync and puns galore,
Together we laugh, forevermore.

Conjoined Dreams

Two heads, one pillow, oh what a sight,
As we dream of cupcakes in the night.
Sailing boats made of cheese and bread,
With jellybean crew members — everyone fed!

Giggling at cats in top hats so spry,
Who juggle fish while they float in the sky.
Whimsical quests weave through our schemes,
In this fusion of giggles, we stitch our dreams.

Dancing with shadows, we plot our pranks,
In a world of silliness that never tanks.
Building castles from sand and ice cream,
This dreamland is where we both gleam.

With a wink and a nudge, we conspire,
In laughter and mischief, we never tire.
Together we leap into realms of cheer,
In our united jest, there's nothing to fear.

Love's Guiding Light

In a world where odd socks dance,
Two mismatched hearts found a chance.
With a laugh and a wink, they glide,
Like awkward penguins, side by side.

When fortune cookies crack and say,
"Share your fries and never stray!"
They toast with pickles, sip on cheer,
In a tale that goes year to year.

Together they flip pancakes that burn,
Use goofy moves to make hearts turn.
With every stumble, each little mess,
They've built a love that's hard to guess.

In life's grand carnival they play,
With cotton candy skies so gay.
As butterflies burst from their pancakes' flight,
They laugh and love in their guiding light.

Reflections of Togetherness

In the mirror, they both pose,
One grins wide, one just flows.
With a toothy grin and pie on face,
Life's a dance, a silly race.

When timing's off and both trip down,
They land in laughter, lose the frown.
With pizza slices stuck in hair,
They share a laugh, a loving stare.

Their dance moves are a sight to see,
Like tangled spaghetti sets them free.
As echoes of giggles fill the air,
Their quirkiness blooms everywhere.

With every toast and silly pun,
Together, they truly have some fun.
In the mirror of life, they shine so bright,
Bouncing along through day and night.

Fated Encounters

A chance meeting at the donut stand,
He dropped his sprinkles, she took a hand.
With frosted smiles in chocolate delight,
They discovered love in a frosting fight.

As their paths crossed at the cat café,
A furball jumped and caused dismay.
With a laugh, they found a shared dream,
A grand adventure with whipped cream.

Inquirers of oddities, dreamers of fun,
They stumbled together, what a run!
With quirky tales and sweet ice cream,
They've painted life like a vivid dream.

At the station, they missed the train,
Yet laughter echoed, overcoming rain.
With every mishap, they found the spark,
Life's a canvas, ignited by heart.

A Shared Cosmic Rhythm

In a universe that spins around,
Two clumsy dancers lost but found.
Stepping on toes, they twirl and sway,
With a rhythm that's uniquely okay.

When pizza gets tossed like a comet fly,
They grab a slice, both laugh and sigh.
With starlit eyes and silly cheers,
They conquer life through giggles and tears.

Bursting forth in a cosmic race,
Skating on laughter, they find their place.
With unexpected twirls and a playful spin,
They embrace the chaos that love brings in.

As meteors streak across the sky,
They leap in unison, oh my, oh my!
With a gentle chuckle, they waltz through night,
Two hearts in laughter, that's their delight.

The Dance of Fates

In a crowded room, we both trip and fall,
Laughing so hard, we forget it all.
My drink spills over, yours lands on your shoe,
Together we giggle, like we always do.

Twisting and spinning, all awkward and bright,
Two left feet moving in a hilarious sight.
We bump into strangers, it's a comical plot,
In this grand ballet, we're giving all we've got.

With each little fumble and each silly glance,
Who knew we'd find romance in this feeble dance?
So let's spin like tops, till we both lose control,
For in this mad jig, we both find our role.

As the music fades, we share our applause,
Our two crazy hearts, sharing laughter's cause.
In life's funny ballet, we'll dance 'til we drop,
Two beings in sync, and we never will stop.

Intertwined Journeys

You took the wrong bus, ended up at my door,
I thought it was fate, we'd never met before.
You said, "Oops, my bad!" with a grin on your face,
I snorted my drink; we're a laugh-out-loud case.

Wandering together down this silly old street,
Dodging pigeons and ducks, we laugh on our feet.
You slip on a banana, I try not to scream,
As we both tumble down, it's just like a dream.

Every wrong turn leads us deeper in fun,
Like two clumsy squirrels chasing after the sun.
With backpacks and snacks, we set out to explore,
Navigating this journey, who could ask for more?

Our paths may be twisted, but we'll find our way,
Spinning in circles, come night or come day.
For in every misstep and every little fall,
We forge a great bond, that conquers it all.

When Hearts Align

In a coffee shop, you steal my last sip,
I raise an eyebrow; you flash a quick flip.
With smiles and giggles over pastries galore,
We craft our own magic, who could ask for more?

Slurping our drinks, we make quite the scene,
Your whipped cream mustache, what a sight, oh so keen!
We ponder on life, invent silly news,
Each laugh that we share feels like we can't lose.

Blushing and grinning under bright café lights,
We blurt out our dreams on those sugar-filled nights.
With every bold story, our spirits take flight,
Two hearts in sync, shining ever so bright.

As the sun sets low, we know this sweet blend,
With laughter and snacks, we've found a true friend.
So pour out the coffee, let laughter consume,
For in this fun space, we both brightly bloom.

Threads of Cosmic Kinship

In a cosmic web, where the stars like to play,
You accidentally text me, what a wacky display!
We share memes and jokes under moonlight's embrace,
Twisting the universe, we've made quite the case.

With alien sightings and oddball requests,
We craft our own worlds, where humor is blessed.
You say, "Let's take space, find a comet to ride!"
And off we embark, on this wild, cosmic slide.

Through planets and asteroids, we laugh all the way,
Navigating this cosmos, it's a fantastic ballet.
So let's gather stardust and dance through the night,
In this intergalactic realm, we both shine so bright.

As we orbit together through laughter and fun,
Who knew that adventure leads both hearts to run?
Two threads in this fabric, so colorful and wild,
In this silly star story, we're forever beguiled.

Love's Interstellar Voyage

In a ship made of cheese and dreams,
We zoom past stars with silly beams.
Your laugh is my rocket fuel,
Floating together, we're nobody's fool.

Eating ice cream in zero gravity,
Your face is a mix of glee and travesty.
With chocolate syrup dripping down,
We orbit the moon, laughing like clowns.

Wormholes twist with a playful glee,
Time bends just for you and me.
We dance on planets made of jelly,
As cosmic jokers with a wiggly belly.

So let's navigate this starry expanse,
With goofy grins and a wobbly dance.
In our cosmic silliness, we stand tall,
Together we'll conquer it all!

A Dance Across Time

With polka dots and boogie shoes,
We waltz through years, no time to lose.
A tango with socks that don't quite match,
Our rhythm is a delightful patch.

We spin through eras with just one glance,
A leap through the ages to a funny dance.
Top hats and feather boas in tow,
Laughing loudly till our cheeks glow.

In the roaring twenties, we're the main act,
With flapper dresses and a dog that's packed.
Time-traveling jester, that's our role,
Dancing our way to a heart and a goal.

So twirl with me under the moonlight,
Each hour that passes feels just right.
With giggles as our timeless call,
Together, we'll always have a ball!

Shared Footprints in the Sand

On sunny shores with ice cream in hand,
We write our tales in the warm, soft sand.
With silly hats and sandals askew,
Our footprints twirl in a bubbly queue.

Seagulls squawk in a jealous fit,
As we build castles that just won't sit.
A sandcastle throne, oh what a sight,
Our royal laughter echoes in the night.

When waves crash down with a foamy grin,
Our footprints vanish, but we begin again.
Jumping high when the tide retreats,
With giggles and splashes, life's little treats.

So let's chase crabs and twirl like stars,
Dancing together beneath our bright Mars.
With laughter, our legacy will expand,
As we continue to wander this crazy land!

The Unfolding of Us

Like origami swans in a breeze,
We fold and crease with playful ease.
Making shapes from paper hearts,
Laughing at all our clumsy starts.

Our stories stack like a tower of books,
With goofy illustrations and funny hooks.
Every page turns with a chuckle and cheer,
Together we write, letting go of fear.

In a universe of mismatched socks,
We skip around like a pair of clocks.
Ticking and tocking in perfect sync,
Creating moments that make us think.

So here's to the laughter, the journeys we chart,
Unfolding our lives, one silly part.
With a wink and a smile, let's embrace the throng,
In the unfolding of us, we always belong!

Harmonious Destinies

In a land where socks go to hide,
We twirl like dancers, side by side.
Our quirks collide, a perfect storm,
Like mismatched shoes, we break the norm.

With pizza slices shared on a bench,
You laugh so hard, you start to wrench.
Like two old clowns in their best show,
We bumble through life, stealing the glow.

Through tickles and odd, funny quirks,
We navigate life's silly works.
In a world where chaos makes us leap,
We find the joy in that goofy heap.

Together we juggle our wild dreams,
Like two lost puzzle pieces, it seems.
In our little circus, we take the lead,
With laughter and love, we plant the seed.

Two Threads Woven

In a room where the curtains sway,
We weave our tales in a funny way.
Your quirks like thread, mine like glue,
A stretch of fabric, just me and you.

With breakfast spills and coffee fights,
We spin our yarn in the morning lights.
Like mismatched mittens, snug but loose,
Tangled up in the daily moose.

We tie our fates with silly bows,
And dance with ants in our snazzy clothes.
In our patchwork life, we find delight,
Like fireworks that light up the night.

Our stitches may fray, but that's just fine,
We laugh at the seams that cross each line.
In this grand fabric, we strut and twirl,
Each loop and twist is our goofy whirl.

In the Presence of Stars

Under moonlit skies, we act bizarre,
Chasing our dreams, no matter how far.
With capes made of bedsheets, we take flight,
Sailing through giggles into the night.

We trade our secrets with slumbering trees,
While sharing popcorn with the buzzing bees.
Each star above winks with glee,
As we plot our next escapade, you and me.

On a comet of laughter, we zip and zoom,
With hiccuping stars in their cosmic bloom.
Like jolly jesters in a celestial game,
Every twinkle giggles and calls our name.

In this vast universe, we make our mark,
Dancing with shadows until it's spark.
With silly wishes upon midnight stars,
We craft our tales from Venus to Mars.

Journeys Intersected

On a train of silliness, we chug along,
With snacks in hand, we can't go wrong.
Each station sings a comical tune,
As we plot our next mischief by the moon.

With each silly hiccup that we narrate,
Our laughter echoes, it's never too late.
Like two clowns riding a tandem bike,
We stumble and giggle as just one hike.

Through puddles and giggles, we leap and bound,
With each twist and turn, adventure is found.
In our merry chase through life's silly maze,
We dance with fate in a joyful craze.

So let's keep chugging on this wild ride,
With snacks and laughter always beside.
In this travelogue of whimsical glee,
We'll write our story, just you and me.

Inseparable Threads of Light

In a world spun by fate's silly hands,
We weave our quirks in mismatched bands.
Your sock on my foot, quite the fashion,
With laughter that sparks endless passion.

Like two peas tossed in a rather odd stew,
Who knew chaos could feel like a zoo?
You drop your ice cream, I slip on a shoe,
Together we tumble—what else can we do?

Tangled in dreams, a delightful dance,
Tripping on jokes, a clumsy romance.
Our giggles echo in the starlit night,
In a universe where wrong feels so right.

So here's to our trip, oh what a wild ride,
With you by my side, I take it in stride.
With each silly mishap, I daresay we find,
That laughter's the thread that ties heart and mind.

Together Against the Tide

In a boat with holes, we set sail today,
Paddling backward in a comical way.
You splash and I giggle, the sea all aglow,
Our mission? To conquer the waves as they flow.

The dolphins tease us, they swim like a breeze,
While seagulls join in for their share of the cheese.
With a bucket of hopes and a spoonful of glee,
We sail through the chaos, just you and me.

Bailing out water with a pancake flip,
You wink and I wonder if we'll ever grip.
As the tide pulls us under, our hearts start to soar,
In this silly adventure, we always want more.

So let's raise a toast with a chocolate fondue,
To the whirlpools of life, out at sea, just us two.
For every wild wave that splashes our pride,
Together we're anchored, come laugh at the ride!

Celestial Signs of Togetherness

Under a sky full of winking stars,
We spot constellations riding in cars.
Your elbow's a comet, my foot's a black hole,
Two dorks in the cosmos playing their role.

Each twinkle above is a wink from the night,
Guiding us home with their shimmering light.
You read the horoscopes and laugh at mine,
While I chase my dreams through your mess of divine.

In a galaxy where giggles collide,
Our orbits entwined in this universal ride.
With every misstep, we create our own spark,
A cosmic ballet, igniting the dark.

So here's to our journey across endless space,
Floating through laughter in this starry place.
With cosmic chaos, I'll always insist,
You're my funny fate, in a galaxy kissed.

Navigating the Constellation of Hearts

In a boat made of wishes, we both take a chance,
Riding the tides of our whimsical dance.
You steer the ship with a jellyfish lead,
While I navigate dreams like a confused kid.

Maps aren't our style, we chart with a smile,
Finding treasure in laughter, mile after mile.
You drop the compass, I humor the fool,
Together we make our own kind of rule.

When storms come a-knocking, we hide in a hug,
Turning worries to jokes while we dance like a bug.
With hearts that are sparkly and quite the delight,
We sail through the chaos from morning to night.

So here's to our voyage, you matey of mine,
In this sea of the silly, our hearts intertwine.
With giggles as lanterns igniting our way,
We're sailing through life in our own quirky ballet.

Twinned Paths Through Time

In a world where socks go missing,
We trip through life, never hissing.
With mismatched shoes and silly hats,
We laugh and dance with the chitchats.

When dinner turns to burnt surprise,
We share a look, then both just cry.
Starlit picnics gone awry,
Yet still we nibble, laugh, and sigh.

In cosmic jest, fate swaps our fate,
Each blunder mocks, yet feels so great.
With tangled blankets and lost keys,
We find our way, just like the bees.

Through time's own lens, we twist and shout,
In goofy styles, there's never doubt.
No need for compass, maps, or maps,
For every turn brings playful laughs.

Guided by Seraphs

When life hands us an awkward fate,
We dance in sync, perhaps too late.
Like angels lost on a pizza quest,
With toppings strange, we do our best.

Silly whispers from up above,
Suggesting we eat chocolate with love.
And when we trip over the air,
Those seraphs giggle, saying, 'Don't care!'

Mismatched rhythms, yet we groove,
In cosmic chaos, our hearts improve.
They guide our steps, with snacks in tow,
In heavenly kitchens, we steal the show.

So here's to jesters in the sky,
With laughter loud, we soar and fly.
As long as you are by my side,
Every blunder feels like a ride.

Beneath the Same Sky

With every sunbeam, a slapstick plot,
Underneath beams, we find a lot.
Kites that tangle and feathers that fall,
We share our giggles, our humorous call.

Clouds play hide and seek again,
As we chase rainbows, my goofy friend.
With ice cream drips down our funny shirts,
Every mishap adds to our quirks.

The moon winks at our comical plight,
As stars share jokes that tickle the night.
We're cosmic fools with hearts so bold,
Collecting moments that never get old.

In this circus of fate that we roam,
Your laughter makes every place feel like home.
With every twinkle of the night sky,
We dance as jesters, you and I.

The Tapestry of Us

In the fabric of quirks, we stitch our tale,
With threads of laughter, we shall prevail.
We weave in blunders, a patchwork bright,
With a splash of chaos, our hearts take flight.

Every hiccup becomes a thread,
We laugh through the mess, no need for dread.
Like mismatched socks, we find our way,
As fabric unfolds, come what may.

From tangled yarns to silly string,
Our tapestry blooms, oh the joy it brings!
With every loop, unplanned and fun,
Our masterpiece sparkles, two becoming one.

So here's our quilt, with stains and cheer,
In every giggle, you hold me dear.
With colors bright and patterns true,
Life's goofy fabric is me and you.

A Canvas of Interwoven Dreams

In a shop of mismatched socks,
They waltzed like wayward clocks.
One tripped over a bubblegum shoe,
And laughter joined the sweet déjà vu.

With crayons drawn from an endless sea,
They painted rainbows that would never be.
Each brushstroke a giggle, bright and bold,
Tales of two with a twist of gold.

A pickle dance in the pouring rain,
They joked of love as a silly game.
Chasing after clouds made of whipped cream,
Echoes of laughter in a whimsical dream.

And when they fell into the cheese fountain,
They splashed around like a joyful mountain.
In the mess of life, they'd find their quest,
With silly grins, they knew they were blessed.

The Unfolding of Sacred Journeys

On a road paved with jellybeans,
They strutted like royalty in fancy jeans.
Each step a moonwalk, oh what a sight,
With ketchup rain and mustard light.

They plotted stars on a paper napkin,
Conspiring with the world's best captain.
With giggles that echoed through the night,
Dreams set sail, with hearts feeling light.

Frogs in boots danced at every twist,
With secret maps hidden in a mist.
Each corner a giggle, each turn a cheer,
Together they ventured, with not a fear.

The world became a bouncy castle,
As they jumped around to a silly rascal.
Hand in hand, they'd stumble and sway,
In the dance of life, they'd sway away.

Bound by Celestial Threads

In the fabric of fate, they wove their tale,
With stitches of laughter that would never pale.
A cosmic yarn spun from playful light,
Together they glittered in the moonlight.

By the sun's rays, they'd twirl a dance,
Spinning the universe into a trance.
Each comet a joke, each star a grin,
In the grand tapestry, they'd always win.

With their quirky hats and mismatched shoes,
They swapped funny dreams like old news.
Their laughter echoed on a merry breeze,
Sowing joy like bright daisies in trees.

As the universe chuckled with glee,
They made their mark like a wild, free spree.
With celestial threads that no one could sever,
In the fabric of life, they danced forever.

Unspoken Harmonies

In the silence, their giggles spoke,
As they plotted mischief and funny jokes.
With cups of laughter, a banquet of cheer,
They crafted a world where joy was near.

Like peanut butter and jelly on toast,
Together they played, a harmonious boast.
With wacky tunes and some silly rhymes,
They danced through life without any crimes.

In the park, they did a tightrope walk,
Made of spaghetti, oh how they'd talk!
With each silly mishap, they'd laugh and sway,
Unspoken harmonies led them astray.

In the quirks of fate, they found their song,
A melody where silly things belong.
With every giggle, every grin wide,
They journeyed through life, side by side.

Entwined Hearts in Cosmic Dance

In a galaxy of shoes, they meet,
Tripping over stars, oh what a feat!
Gravity grins, pulling them near,
While comets chuckle, 'Oh dear, oh dear!'

Salsa with meteors, a wild romance,
Falling through space in a clumsy dance.
With each twirl, they spin and collide,
Ecos of laughter, they can't hide.

Asteroids laugh at their silly plight,
As the cosmos giggles at their delight.
Waltzing through nebulae, hand in hand,
Creating their rhythm, an offbeat band.

The universe blinks, hiding its glee,
At two starry-goofballs, flying carefree.
In their joy, they find a spark,
Creating constellations that light up the dark.

Threads of Fate Woven Together

A tapestry spun from a bright, yarn ball,
Laughter echoes through each thread and thrall.
Knots twist and turn in colors so bright,
As chaos and giggles become pure delight.

Fate's needle pokes, 'Oops, that's my foot!'
While stitches giggle at each little toots.
A blanket of quirks, oh what a sight,
In the fabric of friendship, they shine so bright.

With each new twist, they create more tales,
Of fumbles and blunders, like comical gales.
They weave together, cackling with glee,
A patchwork of joy, just wait and see.

The loom whispers secrets, old tales retold,
Of laughter and warmth, a bond to behold.
In this funny saga, they're always a pair,
Creating a quilt that swirls through the air.

The Meeting of Kindred Spirits

At a quirky café, where the coffee's quite bold,
Two hearts collide, just like stories told.
With donuts and giggles, a vibrant array,
Mismatched socks dancing in a funny ballet.

One spills a latte, oh what a mess,
The other just laughs, 'Well, I must confess!'
They share silly secrets over cookies and tea,
And burst into fits, oh the joy to agree!

With puns and bad jokes, they brighten the space,
In their whirlwind of laughter, they both feel the grace.
As the world whirls around, it's just them in sight,
Two friends on a quest, a bond of pure light.

In this whimsically woven, delightful tête-à-tête,
Every moment's a dance they'll never forget.
With crumbs on their shirts, hearts racing for fun,
Together they sparkle, a wild, carefree run.

Whispers Across the Infinite

In whispers of stars, those silly chums,
They plot funny schemes, and giggle like drums.
Trading jokes in photons that fly,
As the cosmos chuckles, 'Oh my, oh my!'

The sky giggles softly, throwing in spark,
While planets roll over, and chuckle in the dark.
Comets join in with a glittering cheer,
'What a duo, comrades, let's spread some cheer!'

Through the vastness of space, on whimsical trails,
They concoct goofy plans and absurd little tales.
With wishes and winks, they send their delight,
Creating a ruckus in the velvet night.

The universe spins, with a smile on its face,
As these two goofballs explore time and space.
In the echo of laughter, they forever remain,
Whispering joy in an infinite chain.